STUDY GUIDE
for
MAKING ROOM

STUDY GUIDE
for
MAKING ROOM

Recovering Hospitality as a
Christian Tradition

Christine D. Pohl and Pamela J. Buck

William B. Eerdmans Publishing Company
Grand Rapids, Michigan / Cambridge, U.K.

© 2001 Wm. B. Eerdmans Publishing Co.
All rights reserved

Wm. B. Eerdmans Publishing Co.
255 Jefferson Ave. S.E., Grand Rapids, Michigan 49503 /
P.O. Box 163, Cambridge CB3 9PU U.K.

Printed in the United States of America

06 05 04 03 02 01   7 6 5 4 3 2 1

Library of Congress Cataloging-in-Publication Data

Pohl, Christine D.
        Study guide for Making room: recovering hospitality as a Christian tradition /
    Christine D. Pohl and Pamela J. Buck.
            p.   cm.
        Includes bibliographical references.
        ISBN 0-8028-4989-X (pbk.: alk. paper)
        1. Hospitality — Religious aspects — Christianity. 2. Christian life.
    I. Buck, Pamela J.   II. Pohl, Christine D. Making room.   III. Title.

BV4647.H67 P66 2001
241'.671 — dc21

                                                    2001040536

www.eerdmans.com

CONTENTS

ACKNOWLEDGMENTS

Recognition that hospitality is a central practice of the Christian life has been growing over the past several years. As faithful Christians have become familiar with the biblical, theological, and practical importance of offering hospitality to strangers, they have asked for tools to assist them in teaching and discussing the topic. The Study Guide to *Making Room* provides a variety of ways that people can learn more about the practice.

Numerous students at Asbury Theological Seminary contributed to the Study Guide. In two classes on "The Ethics of Hospitality," students offered important suggestions that shaped a number of the questions and activities that have become part of the guide. Special recognition is due to Janet Chilcote, Kurt Crays, Valerie Hattery, and Melynne Rust for their distinctive contributions.

Heartfelt thanks are due to Scott Buck, Martin Gornik, and friends at The Church of the Apostles in Lexington, Kentucky, for their willingness to be coworkers in living out the implications of a commitment to hospitality.

We are also very grateful to Dorothy Bass at the Valparaiso Project for the Education and Formation of People in Faith/Lilly Endowment for her consistent encouragement and practical support and to Dorothy Pohl for her careful reading of the manuscript.

AN INVITATION

"If there is any concept worth restoring to its original depth and evocative potential, it is the concept of hospitality. It is one of the richest biblical terms that can deepen and broaden our insight in our relationships to our fellow human beings."

HENRI NOUWEN[1]

Making Room introduces readers to the richness and the complexity of the hospitality tradition and explores contemporary possibilities for its recovery. By bringing *Making Room* into conversation with biblical texts and with your experiences and understandings of the Christian life, this study guide invites you to make the practice of hospitality part of your daily life and Christian witness.

We have designed the study guide for use by small groups of people who want to understand more about hospitality. The questions are appro-

---

1. Henri Nouwen, *Reaching Out: The Three Movements of the Spiritual Life* (New York: Image Books, 1975), 66.

priate for adult study groups, Sunday school classes, people preparing to undertake a specific social ministry, or a group of friends interested in the topic. This guide can also be used by persons involved in ministries of hospitality to structure reflections on their experiences and to strengthen insights into the practice. For example, those who serve in a soup kitchen or a food pantry, or work with refugees, migrant workers, international students, or Meals on Wheels programs will find opportunities to connect their ministries with the larger tradition of hospitality.

Although designed for a group setting, the study guide could also be used by individuals for personal devotions or spiritual formation.

FORMAT

The guide is divided into nine lessons that correspond to the chapters in *Making Room*. Each lesson begins with a brief introduction to the main points of the book chapter. Sections on group building, Scripture, discussion, reflection, and personal application then follow. These sections have multiple questions from which leaders can choose those most appropriate to their particular group. There are also suggested activities so that participants can address the issues more concretely.

The nine lessons most easily fit into a nine-session series. However, the series could be substantially extended by adding a number of recommended films and activities. It could be shortened to fit a retreat format or a briefer series by reducing the number of topics covered and questions discussed. It is important that, at the beginning of the series, participants agree to a particular time commitment.

Each lesson is composed of the following sections:

- **Group-building Activities.** These assist with group dynamics by helping participants to get to know one another better. The questions provide opportunities to share experiences that encourage more personal discussion of the main concerns of the session.
- **Engaging Scripture.** This section allows participants to deepen their understanding of the significance of hospitality and its particular expressions in the Scriptures.
- **Discussion of the Text.** These questions are tied closely to specific

points or quotations in *Making Room*. They can help the group en-
gage key arguments in the book more critically.

- **Reflection** questions help participants dig deeper into the dynamics
  of hospitality at both the conceptual and the practical level.
- **Personal Experience and Application** bring the ideas in each lesson
  to a more personal and concrete discussion. These questions ask for
  a personal commitment in response to what has been learned.
- **Activities** and **Videos** move the group beyond discussion and provide more concrete and experiential ways of learning. **Full descriptions of each activity are provided at the end of the guide along
  with discussion questions for the recommended videos.**

SUGGESTIONS FOR GROUP LEADERS

Read *Making Room* and the study guide completely before beginning the
study.

Before each meeting, read the relevant chapter and look over the
discussion questions for that lesson. Think about the interests, goals, and
experiences of group members and choose from among the questions
those you think are most appropriate. Try to use something from each
section to accommodate participants' various learning styles. There are
far more questions and activities than can or should be used in a single
session. Thoughtful engagement with a few of the questions will often
cover many of the issues raised by other questions.

Alternative: If each person in your group has a copy of the study
guide, participants could use the guide to structure their individual reading of *Making Room*. When the group gathers, the leader could invite
members to suggest questions for discussion.

Many of the suggested activities require some advance preparation
or involve several sessions to complete. It might be helpful to read
through the **Activities** and **Videos** sections as you begin the study. Identify key activities that would be significant in your setting and note the
time and resources needed. Incorporate these factors into your scheduling
of the study.

It is important to create an environment in which each person's
contributions are encouraged and valued. **Urge the group members to**

come to the meeting having read the relevant chapter in the book so all will have a common vocabulary and background for the discussion.

POSSIBLE ACTIVITIES OVER THE COURSE OF THE STUDY

- Sharing a meal together is particularly appropriate to the topic of hospitality. Throughout the study, group members could have regular potluck suppers or take turns providing meals. During these meals, participants might also share stories of hospitality.
- Prayer is central to the hospitality tradition. Begin or end each session with prayer specifically related to the topic of hospitality and strangers.
- A number of films effectively portray hospitality themes and practices. A brief description and a set of discussion questions for each film are included at the end of the study guide. The group may want to intersperse chapter discussions with films.
- Some of the best learning occurs as people connect their studies with actual expressions of hospitality. Group members could volunteer to work in a soup kitchen or with a refugee agency during the study and reflect on their experiences each week during the shared meal or the discussion.
- Suggested prayers, hymns, and readings are provided at the end of the study guide. The group could use the material to open and close its study sessions or to develop a worship service around the theme of hospitality.

1. INTRODUCTION: A NEW LOOK
AT AN OLD TRADITION

In ancient times, hospitality was viewed as a pillar on which the moral structure of the world rested. It included welcoming strangers into the home and offering them food, shelter, and protection. Providing hospitality also involved recognizing the stranger's worth and common humanity. Hospitality is an important theme in Scripture and is central to the gospel story itself. Both rewarding and challenging, hospitality remains an important expression of Christian faith today.

Major Points of the Chapter

- The distinctively Christian contribution to the hospitality tradition is its emphasis on welcoming the vulnerable, the poor, and the needy.
- The most vulnerable strangers are those people who are disconnected from relationships with family, church, economy, and civic community.
- Hospitality has biblical and early church roots; a fuller awareness of

the tradition enriches faith and brings Christian practice into closer alignment with concerns of the Kingdom.

• Hospitality is a skill, gift, spiritual obligation, and also a practice.

Group-building Activities

1. Invite participants to share with the group why they were drawn to the study and how they hope to benefit from the discussions.

2. Ask group members to share their responses to reading the first chapter. Encourage participants to identify one idea that particularly spoke to them.

Engaging Scripture

1. Read Luke 14:12-14. Reflect on the differences between this picture of hospitality and contemporary images of hospitality.

2. What kinds of people does Jesus welcome (e.g., Mark 10:46-52; Luke 5:27-32, 18:15-17)? Invite the group to think of other passages that provide clues into those welcomed by Jesus.

Discussion of the Text

1. Henri Nouwen wrote that hospitality conjures up images of "tea parties, bland conversation, and a general atmosphere of coziness" (*Making Room*, page 3). John Calvin promised that "no duty can be more pleasing or acceptable to God" than hospitality to religious refugees (*MR*, 6). What do the differences between these two quotes tell us about hospitality today?

2. Philip Hallie suggests that "The opposite of cruelty is not simply freedom from the cruel relationship, it is hospitality" (*MR*, 12). Discuss why eliminating cruelty is not enough for a full human life. In

what ways can hospitality help a victim of cruelty move toward healing?

3. "Strangers, in the strict sense, are those who are disconnected from basic relationships that give persons a secure place in the world. The most vulnerable strangers are detached from family, community, church, work, and polity" (*MR*, 13). Who are such strangers in your neighborhood or community? Discuss what might be required to help these people find a place.

Reflection

1. Discuss the images of hospitality we encounter every day. How have these images shaped our understandings of hospitality? In what ways would a Christian understanding of hospitality challenge our regular practices?

2. There are a number of reasons why offering hospitality to strangers can be difficult. Why is it sometimes also difficult to offer hospitality to family, friends, and acquaintances?

3. We can minister in many different ways to people in need. Often those of us with resources can write a check to a charitable organization. Christian hospitality demands much more of us. What does it involve?

Personal Experience and Application

1. Share personal experiences of wonderful hospitality. What were the components? Were you a stranger, guest, or host? Who has made room for you? When have you made room for someone?

2. What are some of your fears or uncertainties about welcoming strangers?

3. What simple acts of welcome could you begin this week? What small change could you make in your daily routine to become more hospitable?

Activities   *(see Activities section beginning on page 45 for explanations)*

Graffiti Wall
Post-A-Quote
Praying for Strangers

Videos   *(see Videos section beginning on page 54 for descriptions of films and discussion questions)*

Martin the Cobbler
The Visitor

2. ANCIENT AND BIBLICAL SOURCES

The biblical tradition is a rich resource for understandings of hospitality. Images of God as gracious and generous host are found throughout the Scriptures. Writers in the New Testament portray Jesus as a vulnerable guest, a needy stranger, and a gracious host. Jesus both welcomes and needs welcome. For the early church, hospitality was crucial to its survival, identity, and growth.

Major Points of the Chapter

- Because of Jesus' teaching and practice, the Christian hospitality tradition emphasizes welcoming the most vulnerable and poor.
- Jesus not only welcomes the needy but is actually welcomed in them: "Lord, when did we see YOU hungry?"
- In the biblical stories of hospitality, God is often present in surprising ways.
- The people of God are challenged to see themselves as strangers who welcome strangers.

- Jesus' roles as our host and our guest enrich and complicate Christian understandings of hospitality.
- Shared meals and the Eucharist are at the center of Christian hospitality.
- At its best, Christian hospitality is the setting for crossing social boundaries and for healing cultural divisions.
- Hospitality often involves small acts of sacrificial love and service which are important to both giver and recipient.

Group-building Activity

Briefly tell the story of a memorable family holiday or celebration. Discuss how often these included strangers or unexpected circumstances.

Engaging Scripture

1. Read the story of Abraham, Sarah, and the angels in Genesis 18. Discuss the acts of hospitality shown to the strangers. Where in the story did Abraham and Sarah discover their guests' identities? Was their hospitality changed by this revelation? Read Hebrews 13:2 and discuss.

2. Read through the following passages: Matthew 11:28-30; Mark 10:13-14; Luke 5:27-32, 9:10-17, 19:1-10, 22:7-30, and 24:13-35. What does each passage reveal about Jesus' practice of hospitality?

3. Review the explicit New Testament teachings on hospitality (Romans 12:13; Hebrew 13:2; 1 Peter 4:9; 1 Timothy 3:2; Titus 1:8). Who is responsible for hospitality? What do we learn about its practice?

Discussion of the Text

1. Matthew 25:31-46 ("I was a stranger and you welcomed me. . . . Just as you did it to one of the least of these who are members of my fam-

ily, you did it to me") is the most important biblical text for Christian hospitality. Practitioners of hospitality often speak of seeing Jesus in the people in the soup line, seeing Jesus through their dirty clothes and broken spirits, seeing Jesus "in distressing disguise." Dorothy Day wrote about her encounter with Jesus in a homeless man, "There He was, homeless. Would a church take Him in today — feed Him, clothe Him, offer Him a bed? I hope I ask myself that question on the last day of my life" (*MR*, 22). Are there times when you see Jesus in the "least of these"? What difference does it make?

2. "A shared meal is the activity most closely tied to the reality of God's Kingdom, just as it is the most basic expression of hospitality" (*MR*, 30). Do you see the Eucharist/Lord's Supper as a significant expression of hospitality? How is the hospitality we receive at God's table connected to the hospitality we offer?

3. "Hospitality to needy strangers distinguished the early church from its surrounding environment. Noted as exceptional by Christians and non-Christians alike, offering care to strangers became one of the distinguishing marks of the authenticity of the Christian gospel and of the church" (*MR*, 33). In our skeptical culture, how might our caring responses toward strangers help people believe that the claims of Christianity are true?

4. Living in and with the biblical stories, while practicing hospitality, brings the texts alive in remarkable ways. One former seminary student observed that "the scriptures make more sense" as hospitality is lived out (*MR*, 34). Share stories of events that brought new life to a particular Scripture passage. How was your understanding of that text changed by your experience?

Reflection

1. While we should offer hospitality with no expectation that we will benefit from it, are there rewards? What do the biblical texts suggest?

2. Why should we welcome strangers? Is it only for their sakes? Why or why not?

3. How do the biblical stories of hospitality change the way we look at hospitality and ministry to those in need?

4. In what ways does the ambiguity of Jesus as both host and guest challenge our thinking about hospitality?

5. How is hospitality understood in the church today? How does this differ from the biblical and historical accounts? Reflect on the significance of these differences.

6. Discuss your understandings of the Lord's Supper/Eucharist. How does your understanding change when hospitality is emphasized?

7. What was the significance of hospitality for the early Christian communities?

8. Why is it important that hospitality involve more than meeting physical needs?

9. While hospitality is essential, not everyone is particularly gifted in this area. In what ways should it or should it not matter if we are "gifted" in the work of hospitality?

Personal Experience and Application

1. Have you ever encountered Jesus "in distressing disguise"? What were your feelings, fears?

2. Identify people in your life who warmly welcome strangers and others in need. What do they do? How are they viewed by other people?

3. Have you ever welcomed a stranger and found that your guest brought you closer to God? What did you learn?

4. Can you think of a situation in your life where applying insights from this week's discussion might really make a difference? Be specific.

Activities   *(see Activities section beginning on page 45)*

Hospitality Interviews
Las Posadas
Mini-Dramas
Volunteer Experience

Videos   *(see Videos section beginning on page 54)*

Babette's Feast
Weapons of the Spirit

3. A SHORT HISTORY OF CHRISTIAN HOSPITALITY

For much of church history, hospitality was offered from within the home or the church. After the Middle Ages, hospitality faded as a significant moral practice, and changes in the household, church, and economy affected understandings of hospitality. Since that time there have been scattered efforts by Christians to recover hospitality as a central dimension of faithful living.

Major Points of the Chapter

- In biblical times welcoming strangers was both a personal and a community responsibility.
- Hospitality, especially concerns about caring for the poor and strangers, gave rise to hospitals, hospices, and other specialized institutions.
- Care for poor people and poor strangers became more anonymous, less personal.
- Increasingly, hospitality became synonymous with entertaining — a way of displaying wealth and reinforcing power and status.

Group-building Activity

As a group, draw out the time line described in Chapter 3 of *Making Room*. Identify the major time periods and use a few words to describe what hospitality looked like in each era. Note also the key events that affected the practice of hospitality. On the time line, locate where the responsibility for hospitality rested and how that responsibility shifted over time.

Engaging Scripture

1. Old Testament stories of Abraham and Sarah, Lot, etc., demonstrate the importance of individual hospitality to strangers at one's door. Old Testament law made care for strangers and the poor also a communal responsibility. Read Leviticus 19:9-10 and Deuteronomy 14:28-29. Who in the life of Israel needed special care and why? What provisions were made for sojourners?

2. Read the story of the Shunammite woman and Elisha in 2 Kings 4:8-37. Discuss the location and components of the hospitality offered by the woman and her husband. How did Elisha respond? This is one of the key passages for later instructions to establish a "prophet's chamber" or "Christ room" in one's home.

Discussion of the Text

1. John Chrysostom, a church leader from the fourth and early fifth centuries, established some of the first institutions to help Christians provide hospitality to large numbers of people. However, he worried that hospitality was also an individual's personal responsibility (*MR*, 45). What are the advantages and disadvantages of a more institutionalized approach to hospitality? What is lost and gained when Christian hospitality is seen as "public service" (*MR*, 43)?

2. By the eighteenth century in the Western world, hospitality had almost disappeared as a significant Christian practice. Although John

Wesley recovered many aspects of ancient hospitality, he did not call those activities "hospitality" (*MR*, 55). How did this contribute to the loss of the historic tradition? Is the name we give to a practice important?

3. In the past, settings which brought together church and household fostered a hospitality that broke down significant social boundaries, such as class and ethnic differences. "The overlap of household and church combines the most personal level of interaction with the most significant institutional base for transcending social differences and creating community" (*MR*, 56). What makes this overlapping space unique? How can we be more intentional about creating similar space for hospitality today?

4. Look at the time line created in the **Group-building Activity** above:
    a. Discuss the intentions of the changes when they were initiated.
    b. Reflect on the unforeseen consequences over time.
    c. How do you think it would feel to be a host in these periods? To be a guest?
    d. What do you learn from the locations of hospitality in the various periods?

Reflection

1. Why was hospitality so important in the first centuries of the church? Are there ways it is similarly important today?

2. What settings for hospitality are important today? What makes a place good for hospitality?

3. Do we worry about social status in offering hospitality today? How does hospitality remain helpful in reinforcing relationships, power, and status?

4. Often hospitality has been viewed primarily as a woman's task. Because of the commitment and work involved, any effort to recover

hospitality could be very burdensome for women. Why is hospitality seen as a woman's responsibility? Is such a view true to biblical teaching? What contemporary gender concerns need to be addressed in recovering hospitality?

Personal Experience and Application

1. Think of recent experiences when you were a guest. Describe the settings and the institutions involved. How often did you pay for hospitality services?

2. When you think of welcoming needy strangers today, where would that usually occur?

3. What could you do better to connect your church and home life to create space for welcoming strangers?

4. What makes home-based hospitality difficult or worrisome today? What makes it important?

5. Can you think of a time that you did not respond to someone's need because you thought an agency or organization would take care of her or him? What made offering a personal response difficult? Why might it have been important?

Activities   *(see Activities section beginning on page 45)*

Ethnic Traditions and Celebration
Information Fair
Refugee Ministries
Shared Meals

Video   *(see Videos section beginning on page 54)*

Entertaining Angels: The Dorothy Day Story

4. HOSPITALITY, DIGNITY, AND THE POWER OF RECOGNITION

We express respect when we give and when we receive welcome. Offering hospitality to people who are unimportant in the eyes of the world affirms their value and humanness. Especially when the larger society disregards or dishonors certain persons, respectful gestures and small acts of welcome are potent far beyond themselves. They point to a different system of valuing and an alternate model of how we can relate to one another.

Major Points of the Chapter

- Concerns about equality and human rights have deep roots in ancient Hebrew and Christian commitments to hospitality.
- Hospitality is an expression of friendship; it helps us to see dignity as well as need.
- Eating together expresses acceptance and equality.
- For the Christian tradition, respect for strangers is rooted in the image of God, our common humanity, and in the possibility that Christ might come to us in the form of a stranger.

- Christian history is splattered with failures in hospitality and terrible expressions of exclusion.
- Those who offer hospitality are not so much providing a service as they are sharing their lives with people.

Group-building Activities

1. Reflect on a time you, or a group to which you belong, were treated as if you were unimportant, uninteresting, or simply not there. Imagine what it would feel like if a whole society treated you that way. Relate your feelings to the experiences of people who are homeless or who are living in a nursing home.

2. Describe a time you were in need of help from a stranger. How did you feel about asking for assistance?

Engaging Scripture

1. Read Matthew 25:31-46. At the final judgment, Jesus says to the nations gathered before him, ". . . Inherit the kingdom prepared for you from the foundation of the world; for I was hungry and you gave me food . . . I was a stranger and you welcomed me. . . ." How do the two groups of people respond? Why are they surprised? What does it mean that our welcome into the kingdom is tied to our having offered hospitality to "the least"?

2. Read Luke 14:7-24, especially verses 12 through 14. Identify all the possible reasons that Jesus might tell hosts to invite the poor, the crippled, the lame, and the blind to their dinner parties. Note especially the connection with the Parable of the Great Dinner in verses 15-24.

3. Read the story of the encounter between Jesus and two disciples on the road to Emmaus in Luke 24:13-35. When did the disciples real-

ize that the stranger they had welcomed was Jesus? Why do you think they recognized him "in the breaking of the bread"?

4. Read 1 Corinthians 5:9-13 and 2 John 9-11. In the New Testament, what kinds of people are denied hospitality and why are they excluded from the community? Is it possible to hold church discipline and exclusion in tension with hospitality? Now read the Parable of the Good Samaritan in Luke 10:25-37. What does Jesus say about our response to strangers in need? Is it ever appropriate to deny welcome to people in desperate need?

Discussion of the Text

1. John Calvin attributes dignity to every person, regardless of their neediness, because every person bears God's image and because all persons share the human experiences of vulnerability and dependence (*MR*, 64-66). Why is it important that we have biblical and theological bases for respecting the worth of every person?

2. John Wesley warned his followers to treat the poor with respect and kindness. He said, "If you cannot relieve, do not grieve, the poor. Give them soft words, if nothing else. Abstain from either sour looks or harsh words" (*MR*, 71). How do we sometimes grieve the poor when we refuse to help them? How might we grieve needy people as we provide help?

3. Many practitioners of hospitality comment on their joy and surprise in discovering how much they learned from their guests and how much their guests ministered to them (*MR*, 72). Why is it that the gifts of hospitality do not flow in one direction only?

4. One practitioner, committed to seeking justice and to offering hospitality, observed, "Justice is important, but supper is essential" (*MR*, 74). What is the relationship between eating together and seeking justice?

Reflection

1. In what ways might hospitality be considered resistance? What are we resisting?

2. Who are the people in our society who are invisible? Think about those less apparent than the homeless, such as latchkey children and elderly or handicapped adults. How do people become invisible? Why is it important to a society that some populations stay invisible?

3. A shared meal is often a "leveler" — a time when social differences matter less among people. What personal experiences come to mind that support this statement? How do people protect themselves from this leveling?

4. What are the implications for recognizing Jesus and not recognizing Jesus in strangers? How might this possibility transform your encounters with strangers?

5. How can we offer personal hospitality while respecting significant differences between hosts and guests?

6. How would you communicate that you respect people while you are giving them assistance they really need?

7. We are sometimes more willing to help people than to share our lives with them. Discuss when this is appropriate. Why do we often prefer to serve homeless, elderly, and disabled people, rather than to visit or share a meal with them?

Personal Experience and Application

1. What barriers are in place that keep certain populations invisible? Think about reaching out to someone in one of these groups. What thoughts first come to mind? Feelings?

2. What difficult issues in today's news could be discussed under the heading of hospitality or giving recognition to certain groups of people? Does understanding the conflict as a matter of hospitality change how you interpret the problem?

3. How do you feel about facing Jesus knowing how you and your church have responded to strangers?

4. What do meals mean in your household or church? Are they times for sharing life as well as food?

5. Share stories about how a shared meal helped build community among strangers.

Activities   *(see Activities section beginning on page 45)*

> **Exclusion vs. Embrace Role Play**
> **Graffiti Wall**
> **Shared Meals**
> **Stranger Collage**

Videos   *(see Videos section beginning on page 54)*

> *And Then Came John*
> *Spitfire Grill*
> *Weapons of the Spirit*

5. THE STRANGERS IN OUR MIDST

Strangers are people without a place. To be without a place is to be disconnected from basic, life-supporting institutions — family, work, civil society, and religious community — and to be without the networks of relations that sustain and support human beings. People without a place who also lack financial resources are the most vulnerable people. Such people need generous welcome. But there are many other strangers and neighbors for whom hospitality can also have important benefits.

Major Points of the Chapter

- Throughout much of human history, people have worried about the risks and dangers of welcoming strangers; finding ways to reduce risk is important.
- Not every stranger needs food, clothing, and shelter, but everyone needs friendships and opportunities to contribute their gifts to a community.
- The loss of community and the emphasis on privacy today make it

19

essential that we create threshold places for building relationships with strangers.

Group-building Activities

1. Take turns describing a personal experience of having been a stranger in another culture or in an unfamiliar setting. How did you feel? How did people treat you? What made you most uncomfortable?

2. Tell about a relationship with someone very different from yourself for which you are grateful. Briefly describe how your differences make the relationship more interesting.

3. Share stories from parents and grandparents about when it was "easier" to offer hospitality to strangers.

Engaging Scripture

1. Read Genesis 19:1-3, 1 Kings 17:10-13, Luke 5:27-29, and Acts 16:11-15. All of these passages describe encounters among strangers who eventually go home together. Notice where the conversation first begins. Where do we encounter strangers? Why do we need to pay more attention to places that bridge public and private space?

2. Read Acts 18:27, Romans 16:1-2, and 1 Corinthians 16:3. Discuss how the early church reduced the risk of welcoming strangers into the community. Why was it important that a person known to the community vouch for the faith and contribution of the stranger?

Discussion of the Text

1. "A very potent way to exclude strangers from even the most basic provision and safety, not to mention our homes, is to focus on their

difference and to exaggerate their strangeness" (*MR*, 97). Why is it important to focus on commonalities with strangers? How can we respect people's differences without exaggerating their strangeness or "otherness"?

2. "One of the ways to reduce risk is to make hospitality more public. . . . Welcoming total strangers is difficult when there is no community setting in which initial minimal relations can be established. . . . Hospitality begins at the gate, in the doorway, on the bridges between public and private space. Finding and creating threshold places is important for contemporary expressions of hospitality" (*MR*, 94-95). Identify threshold places in your community, places where strangers can begin talking with one another. What is it about such environments that makes them safe and comfortable? What resources other than space can provide a way to reduce strangeness?

3. In offering hospitality to strangers, bridge or threshold people are very important. "Such persons understand both the world of the stranger and the world of the welcoming community" (*MR*, 95). Who are "bridge people" in your church and community? Why are they good at moving between both worlds?

4. "A steady exposure to distant human need that is beyond our personal response can gradually inoculate us against particular action. . . . Isolation from local need, and overexposure to overwhelming but distant need, make our responses to strangers uncertain and tentative at best" (*MR*, 91). Discuss your responses to media coverage of desperate human crises. Identify ways to connect global and local concerns for the needs of strangers.

Reflection

1. Who are the outsiders in your community? What keeps them "outside"? What do you have in common with them?

2. Why is overcoming strangeness necessary in offering personal hospitality? In what ways do we tend to see those different from us as "bad" or "odd"?

3. Besides making hospitality more public, what other factors reduce risk in welcoming strangers?

4. First steps toward hospitality could include more regularly welcoming family, friends, or church members into our lives and homes. All of us benefit from generous hospitality. How might more experience with welcoming these people make us better at welcoming complete strangers?

5. Often people with children worry about welcoming strangers into their homes. There are both risks and blessings. What could be done to address concerns about children's well-being?

6. Adoption, foster care, and mentoring are all ways of responding to the needs of children in vulnerable situations. How might the hospitality tradition enrich your valuing of these responses?

7. It is often easy to subtly exclude people with disabilities from church. What practices suggest to people that they are not welcome? How can these practices be changed?

8. Describe a cross-cultural situation in which you were trying to be helpful or to exhibit Christ-like responses to a stranger, but because of different values or misunderstandings in communication, you caused hurt or felt frustrated. Did you react by assigning to the other person negative qualities or motives? Identify key elements of the situation. What happened? How did you feel? How was the misunderstanding resolved?

Personal Experience and Application

1. Picture yourself as "without a place." What feelings does this image stir?

2. In what ways are you a "relative stranger" in today's society (*MR*, 89)? Have you moved recently? Do you feel disconnected from family, church, or community? How does this affect your ability and inclination to welcome other strangers?

3. Who are the people around you who are in need of human connections? What factors encourage their isolation? Are there small steps you could take to encourage relationships?

4. What prejudices and attitudes will you have to deal with before you can find certain kinds of strangers interesting?

5. Is welcoming strangers an easy, natural thing for you to do? If yes, what makes it easy? If no, what are your biggest fears or uncertainties?

6. Does your life-style (e.g., where you live, those you spend your time with, what you spend your money on) make it unlikely that you will encounter people in need of hospitality? If you want to be more hospitable, what could you do to open up your life to others?

7. What first steps could you take to make a place in your home or church for children in the neighborhood, teens, elderly neighbors, sick friends, international students, returning missionaries, etc.?

8. Certain situations and certain kinds of strangers make hospitality more difficult (*MR*, 98-100). What groups or situations test your commitment to hospitality? What might you do to make these difficulties more manageable?

Activities *(see Activities section beginning on page 45)*

Ethnic Traditions and Celebration
Mini-Dramas
Praying for Strangers
Shared Meals, especially variations 2 and 3
Stranger Collage

Videos *(see Videos section beginning on page 54)*

And Then Came John
Spitfire Grill

6. HOSPITALITY FROM THE MARGINS

When hospitality involves more than entertaining family and friends, when it helps people cross social boundaries and build community, when it meets significant human needs and reflects divine generosity, we often encounter hosts who are themselves marginal to the larger society.

Major Points of the Chapter

- The most generous hosts have in some way been strangers themselves.
- Hospitality to strangers requires a light hold on possessions and on the need to hide our frailties and weaknesses.
- Gracious hosts are open to recognizing and receiving the gifts of others.
- The role of host often empowers people; it acknowledges that they have something valuable to offer others.

Group-building Activity

Describe an incident in which you felt like the outsider (e.g., a visit to the hospital, changing schools, a trip to a foreign land). What reinforced your feelings of separateness? What part of that experience helped you to be more aware of the needs and feelings of strangers in similar situations?

Engaging Scripture

1. Read Exodus 23:9, Leviticus 19:33-34, and Deuteronomy 10:17-19. Discuss the significance of the Israelites' experience of having been vulnerable strangers in someone else's land. Why was it important that they remember their feelings and experiences? (See also *MR*, 105.)

2. Read Luke 19:1-10. What role does Jesus give to Zacchaeus and what difference does it make? Why does the crowd grumble? How does Zacchaeus respond? Note all the ways that Zacchaeus was affected by the opportunity to welcome Jesus.

Discussion of the Text

1. The most transformative expressions of hospitality are associated with hosts whose social and economic status is unstable, who live on the edges of their society, or who lack clearly defined roles in the important institutions of life (*MR*, 106-112). "Like Jesus, the best hosts are not completely 'at home' themselves, but still make a place of welcome for others" (*MR*, 119). Discuss how a more marginal position helped Christians to be more sensitive to the needs of strangers. How does the marginality of hosts affect the nature of the relationship with needy guests?

2. "Hospitality does not require many resources; it does require a willingness to share what we have, whether food, time, space, or money. It often seems that the most gracious hosts are themselves quite

poor" (*MR*, 116). Why is it that the poorest are often the first to share from their minimal resources? Discuss what enables the poor to give out of their poverty and why those with plenty might be more hesitant to offer hospitality.

3. "When we offer hospitality, our faults as well as our possessions are open to scrutiny. If we need to hide either, we are unlikely to offer much hospitality. Hospitality to strangers . . . has a way of laying bare our lives and surfacing our inadequacies. . . . Hospitality requires a dynamic mix of honest assessments of adequacy, need, and God's sufficiency. . . . Hosts must also be able to move through their own brokenness in order to welcome others" (*MR*, 118). What is it about hospitality that makes our inadequacies more obvious? How can we be honest about our own weaknesses without becoming self-absorbed? In what ways do our weaknesses open up the door to deeper ministry?

Reflection

1. What makes someone a good host?

2. What kinds of activities in the church would provide an opportunity to reverse typical guest and host roles? How might that help empower people who are usually seen as having fewer resources and assets?

3. In our society, how are those who receive assistance viewed and treated? What factors contribute to these attitudes? Which of these factors are characteristic of the people and which are the results of the circumstances in which they find themselves?

4. Often Christians think they need to cover up their frailties in order to do good ministry. What are the good reasons for trying to live beyond our weaknesses? What are the dangers of covering up our inadequacy?

5. Many good hosts deliberately put themselves in positions of vulnerability and marginality. How does a "self-chosen" marginality help us identify with the experiences of those on the margins? How would this experience differ because of the choice involved?

Personal Experience and Application

1. Reflect on the difference between "being present to people" and "problem solving." With which are you more comfortable? As a church community, at which are you more successful? Which do you feel counts more as "real ministry." Why?

2. How are you helped or hindered by your possessions in offering hospitality? Which possessions would be important if you understood hospitality less as entertaining and more as sharing your life?

3. Are you more comfortable as a guest or as a host? Why?

4. In situations where you have been a host, have you been aware of the power associated with that role? How did you use that power? Discuss how a willingness to be a guest of someone else can be an act of ministry in itself.

5. People view churches as sanctuaries *from* the world or as sanctuaries *for* the world. How do you view your church and the property? How does this help or hinder hospitality?

6. In what ways would perceiving yourself as an alien and a stranger in the world change your understanding of Christian discipleship?

Activities   (*see Activities section beginning on page 45*)

    Building on What You Have
    Exclusion vs. Embrace Role Play
    Shared Meals
    Volunteer Experience

Videos   *(see Videos section beginning on page 54)*

Spitfire Grill
Weapons of the Spirit

7. THE FRAGILITY OF HOSPITALITY: LIMITS, BOUNDARIES, TEMPTATIONS

In offering hospitality, practitioners often come face-to-face with the difficulties posed by limited resources. Communities encounter tensions when they simultaneously seek to welcome strangers different from themselves and try to maintain a particular way of life. Because hospitality is a powerful human practice, it can be misused by both guests and hosts.

Major Points of the Chapter

- The goodness and the difficulties of hospitality go hand in hand.
- People who care about hospitality struggle with boundaries and without them.
- Faithful hosts must make choices in distributing resources and in expending energy. Often this means living in the tension between having limited resources and the promise of God's abundance.
- The potential for misuses of hospitality cannot be eliminated. Sometimes our efforts to control abuses undermine the grace that is so important to the practice of hospitality.

Group-building Activity

Take turns telling stories about a time
- when you were denied welcome, when there was no room for you.
- when you had far more guests than you had expected but found that there was sufficient food.

Engaging Scripture

1. Read Exodus 16:4-36 and Matthew 6:25-34. What do these passages suggest about God's provision for us and for our needs?

2. Read John 6:1-14. Reflect on the abundance available when Jesus distributes the bread. What are the implications of this for our expectations as we offer hospitality?

3. Read Acts 15:1-21. What do the apostles decide is necessary in order for the Gentiles to belong to the new Christian community? Why was it such an important issue? What can we learn from this struggle with boundaries and inclusion in the early church?

Discussion of the Text

1. "In offering hospitality, practitioners live between the vision of God's Kingdom in which there is enough, even abundance, and the hard realities of human life in which doors are closed and locked, and some needy people are turned away or left outside. A door — open or closed — is one of the most powerful images of hospitality" (*MR*, 131). Identify some of the reasons a door might be closed. In what situations would it be particularly terrible to deny welcome?

2. "Separation and hospitality are . . . two manifestations of the same love: following Christ and receiving Christ" (*MR*, 139). What are some of the tensions in trying to live a holy life while simulta-

neously providing hospitality to strangers? Why are both practices essential to Christian identity?

3. "To view hospitality as a means to an end, to use it instrumentally, is antithetical to seeing it as a way of life, as a tangible expression of love. . . . When we use occasional hospitality as a tool, we distort it, and the people we 'welcome' know quickly that they are being used" (*MR*, 144-145). In what situations are we tempted to use hospitality for our gain? Why are we so inclined to ask, "What will hospitality accomplish?" How can we resist this misuse of hospitality?

Reflection

1. What kinds of boundaries are worth protecting in your family, church, and community? In what ways does welcoming certain kinds of strangers threaten cherished relationships and cultural practices? Can this involve significant loss? How can we maintain the balance between these risks and the responsibility to welcome strangers?

2. How do faithful Christians handle the tension between generous hospitality and the possibilities of its abuse? What approaches would you use? Why?

3. Brainstorm about how people might set limits without negating the offer of hospitality.

4. Have you seen hospitality used for ambition or for advantage? What did it look and feel like?

5. Our society emphasizes productivity and efficiency. But hospitality takes time and often does not produce measurable results. Discuss the tension among these values. How is this tension handled in some of the situations of hospitality you have encountered or discussed?

6. In your experiences of various forms of outreach to others, was the focus on providing "service" or on building relationships? Was this appropriate to the situation? What could have helped to encourage growth in relationships?

7. Identify the resources that people worry about in offering hospitality in your church setting. Is hospitality approached from a mind-set of abundance or scarcity?

8. What are some differences between "entertaining" and "hospitality"?

Personal Experience and Application

1. Do you sometimes feel that there is not "enough of you" to offer hospitality? Explain.

2. Have you ever felt burned by guests who misused your hospitality? Did that experience make you hesitate to offer welcome again? How did you process that event?

3. Have you experienced God's provision in the midst of significant need? Discuss. Have you had experiences where there were not enough resources to meet the need? Do you think that there is always "enough"?

4. Have you ever had to tell a person that there was no room when welcome was important to her or him? How did you feel? How do we usually avoid having to turn someone away?

5. Have you ever used hospitality for gain or ambition? How can you tell when you are using it for your advantage?

6. Who in your family, community, or church does hospitality (not entertaining) well? How do they handle limits and boundaries?

Activities   *(see Activities section beginning on page 45)*

    Plan Ahead
    Refugee Ministries
    Shared Meals, especially variations 4 and 5

Video   *(see Videos section beginning on page 54)*

    Entertaining Angels: The Dorothy Day Story

8. MAKING A PLACE FOR HOSPITALITY

Concerns about hospitality challenge us to make the places in which we spend our time more welcoming. It is particularly important to pay attention to qualities that make our homes and churches more inviting. Whether or not we can always make room, hospitality begins with dispositions characterized by love and generosity.

Major Points of the Chapter

- Hospitable places are comfortable, safe, and lived in.
- It is crucial to distinguish between "entertaining" and "hospitality."
- Conversations in the context of shared meals are an important practice for families and churches.
- Fellowship is one of the church's best and most overlooked resources.
- Insights from the hospitality tradition can help correct weaknesses in the social service system.

Group-building Activity

Describe a place that is special to you. What makes it special and inviting? If you have an "imagined" place, what does it look (sound, smell) like?

Engaging Scripture

Look at several examples of hospitality in the list below. What are the evidences that hospitality is being offered/received? What details of location and resources are provided? What do these places have in common? What are the differences? Are there any characteristics common to all events?

Genesis 18; 1 Kings 17:8-16; 2 Kings 4:8-37; Luke 8:1-3, 9:1-6, 9:10-17, 24:13-35; John 13:1-20, 21:1-14; Acts 2:42-47.

Discussion of the Text

1. In the fourth/fifth century John Chrysostom urged members of his congregation, "Make for yourself a guest-chamber in your own house: set up a bed there, set up a table there and a candlestick [cp. 2 Kings 4:10]. . . . Have a room to which Christ may come; say, 'This is Christ's cell; this building is set apart for Him.'" Such a room, according to Chrysostom, would be for the "maimed, the beggars, and the homeless" (MR, 154). Discuss how viewing our spare beds or guest rooms as belonging to Christ might affect our decisions about whom we welcome and how we welcome them.

2. "When hospitality is viewed as entertainment, the house is never ready" (MR, 154). How is entertaining different from making people feel welcome and at home? What does worrying about having the "perfect house" say about motives and priorities in hospitality?

3. "Many urban churches have reached out through elaborate and costly programs, but a fence of professional distance remains. They

have not allowed the stranger to be one with them" (*MR*, 159). Discuss how and why churches tend to respond to the needs of strangers and the poor with programs. How might congregations offer the gift of friendship as well as provide assistance to people in need?

4. Some communities of hospitality explicitly distance themselves from social services models that are oriented around the inadequacies or disabilities of their "clients." They try to avoid bureaucratic and highly specialized forms of service and focus instead on the importance of reciprocal relationships within community (*MR*, 160-166). What is at stake in this distinction? Discuss the strengths and weaknesses of each approach. Under what circumstances would one or the other approach be more helpful to persons in need?

Reflection

1. What are the characteristics of a hospitable place? Think about location, furnishings, atmosphere, temperature, odors, noise level, etc.

2. What made it possible for hospitality to be spontaneous and "natural" in the biblical and historical accounts?

3. Do you know people who find it easy to invite others home on the spur of the moment? What are the characteristics of their homes and their lives that make such a practice possible?

4. Is it enough to make room in one's heart for hospitality?

5. How do we use the telephone to offer hospitality? In what ways is it helpful and in what ways does it dilute the hospitality offered?

6. Churches that have not nurtured a common life among members often find it difficult to offer hospitality to strangers. On the other hand, churches that have a rich common life can overlook the importance of offering hospitality to strangers. Discuss the various reasons that hospitality and strangers are problematic in each case.

7. What do intentional communities of hospitality teach us about welcoming strangers?

8. Brainstorm about creative living arrangements that would allow richer hospitality and community among various generations of a family or among families in the church.

9. What settings or events at church encourage hospitality and conversation with others?

10. Besides welcoming people into our homes and churches, in what other settings might we act hospitably?

11. Think about social service agencies with which you have come in contact. Which ones have hospitality and relationship-building as central features? How are such agencies different from standard service providers?

Personal Experience and Application

1. Reflect on meals in your home. What are those times like? Do family members eat together regularly? In your family, do members nourish each other with food and conversation? What minor changes would allow you to accommodate guests more frequently?

2. Do members of your church open their homes to one another? What might you do to encourage this practice?

3. Imagine creating a "Christ room" in your home or in your church. Where would you locate it? How would you furnish it? Who would be your first guests (e.g., your children's friends, troubled teens, friends or neighbors recovering from surgery, international visitors, returning missionaries)?

4. What could you do in your church to make room for hospitality?

5. What might you have to give up in order to make room in your heart/home/church for hospitality?

6. Describe your work environment. What might a commitment to hospitality look like in your job (e.g., as a teacher, salesclerk, bus driver, social worker, police officer, physician, small-business owner, or day-care worker)?

7. Think about your church community. What would a stranger to your church see that confirms your commitment to welcoming Jesus and "the least of these"?

8. More than anything else, vulnerable strangers need connections with other people. What could your local church do to help foster new relationships?

9. How would your life be different if hospitality were a life-style? What steps could you take to move in that direction?

10. Imagine designing a home or church that embodies hospitality or makes hospitality easier. What would it look like?

11. What are the dangers of thinking that the only way to offer hospitality is to get it perfect or to make it beautiful?

Activities   *(see Activities section beginning on page 45)*

Building on What You Have
Hospitality Interviews
Information Fair
Plan Ahead
Praying for Strangers
Shared Meals, especially variation 1
Walk around the Walls

Video   *(see Videos section beginning on page 54)*

Babette's Feast

9. THE SPIRITUAL RHYTHMS OF HOSPITALITY

Hospitality is less a task than it is a way of living our lives and sharing ourselves. Christian hospitality begins with worship and gratitude to God and is cultivated over a lifetime. It emerges from a willingness to make time and space for people.

Major Points of the Chapter

- The difficulties and joys of hospitality lie close together.
- Hospitality must be taught and nurtured, learned and practiced.
- Certain gestures communicate welcome, especially eating together and paying attention to other persons.
- Sustained hospitality requires opportunities for rest and renewal.

Group-building Activities

1. Think of a habit you tried to change. Did you succeed? If not, what would have helped?

2. Look at the **Graffiti Wall** or **Post-A-Quote** you developed during the study. Have each member of the group reflect on what he or she thinks is an important insight.

3. Invite group members to share what they learned from interviewing people who do hospitality well. (See questions under **Hospitality Interviews** in the **Activities** section.)

Engaging Scripture

Read Genesis 2:1-3, Exodus 20:8-11, and Isaiah 58. Reflect on the relationship between hospitality, rest, and worship. Why is it so easy for us to lose any or all of these as priorities in our lives? Discuss how and why they all are essential to the Christian life but difficult to hold in balance.

Discussion of the Text

1. It is easier to make a habit of hospitality when we remember how much Jesus is present in the practice. While we might encounter Jesus in the strangers and guests we welcome, hospitality also allows us to act as Jesus to those guests. Esther de Waal suggests that at the end of all of our hospitable activity, we are faced with two questions, "Did we see Christ in them? Did they see Christ in us?" (*MR*, 173). How might these questions shape our responses to strangers? How might they serve as a spiritual discipline?

2. "Hospitality is one of those things that has to be constantly practiced or it won't be there for the rare occasion" (*MR*, 176). Identify "rare occasions" or emergencies when hospitality is crucial to survival. How would a regular practice of hospitality make these occasions more manageable?

3. "The most precious thing a human being has to give is time," observed one experienced practitioner of hospitality. Another wisely commented, "In a fast food culture, you have to remind yourself

that some things cannot be done quickly" (*MR*, 178). What makes the gift of time so precious? Discuss how you feel about taking time for hospitality.

4. Jean Vanier describes his struggle with offering a person his full attention. "Sometimes when people knock at my door, I ask them in and we talk, but I make it clear to them in a thousand small ways that I am busy, that I have other things to do. The door of my office is open, but the door of my heart is closed" (*MR*, 178-179). Discuss ways that we communicate to people that they are interruptions. Why are some activities defined as tasks and others as interruptions? How do you give someone your full attention even if it is only for a few minutes? If you cannot respond to guests when they first arrive, how can you defer the conversation while still recognizing its value?

Reflection

1. Why is it important to name hospitality as a significant Christian practice? In what ways is telling stories about hospitality crucial to keeping the practice alive?

2. Think of ways that you could learn and collect stories of hospitality. What are some settings in which those stories could be told?

3. What are the dangers of not building rest and worship into hospitality?

4. What gestures communicate to you that you are valued or welcomed? What small acts of hospitality do you regularly practice that people seem to appreciate?

5. Share what you learned from the interviews with people who do hospitality well. What did they say was the best part? What was the hardest? How did they learn the practice?

6. A sense of humor is essential to sustaining hospitality. It is especially important to be able to laugh at ourselves. Share humorous stories concerning hospitality — where the last laugh was on you.

7. How is it possible that hospitality is a command for all Christians, a spiritual gift, and a skill that can be learned? Does it help to see hospitality as a practice and a way of life?

Personal Experience and Application

1. Have you ever been in a position where you had to provide hospitality but you did it grudgingly? How did you feel and behave? How might a grateful spirit have made a difference?

2. What factors in your life keep you from offering hospitality to strangers?

3. What are you already doing that you could build on in your home, church, and community? What changes would you need to make in your life, family, and church in order to become more hospitable?

4. How do you handle the tension between things that interrupt your schedule and the fact that interruptions are frequently opportunities for hospitality?

5. What evidence is there that your children are learning to be hospitable? What could you do to nurture them toward hospitality?

6. The testimony of many people who offer hospitality is that they "received more than they gave" (*MR*, 186). Share stories in which this was your experience.

7. Take time individually to write out three things that over the next three months you will do to make hospitality a way of life. Share these with the group and devise a way of holding one another accountable for the next several months.

Activities   *(see Activities section beginning on page 45)*

    Las Posadas
    Shared Meals

Videos   *(see Videos section beginning on page 54)*

    Martin the Cobbler
    The Visitor

ACTIVITIES

Building on What You Have

Identify a service provided in your church or in your community. Find ways a commitment to hospitality could shift the model of helping from "service" to friendship. For example, a church that has a Mother's Morning Out program could expand it slightly and offer hospitality to the mothers who come by providing a place for coffee and conversation.

Ethnic Traditions and Celebration

Invite people from a particular ethnic group in your community to talk to your church group about their traditions and how they preserve them. Work together to make plans to co-sponsor a traditional celebration that would include both communities.

Exclusion vs. Embrace Role Play[2]

Write out each situation described below on an individual card. Make another set of cards, half of which say "exclude" and half, "embrace." Mix the "exclude/embrace" cards. Stack both sets and place them facedown. Divide the participants into groups of three or four people. Have a member of each group take one card from the "situation" stack and one from the "exclude/embrace" stack. Have the groups take turns reading their situation card out loud and then acting out the situation with the attitude of exclusion or embrace. Reflect on the gestures that communicate welcome or rejection, and respect or disrespect. Discuss the feelings about being excluded or included that are stirred by participating in and observing the skits.

Situations

1. You are walking down the street and need to pass several homeless people huddled in a building entrance and asking for handouts.

2. You go to pick up your friend at her place of employment, a sheltered workshop for mentally handicapped adults. You enter her room where several clients are working. One is in a wheelchair, one has Down's syndrome, and one who doesn't speak has problems with drooling. Your friend's aide hasn't come back to the room, so she asks you to stay while she goes to find the aide. One of the clients begins a conversation with you but you don't understand his/her speech.

3. A member of your church who has been experiencing severe depression for the past few months has missed worship for several weeks in a row. You run into each other at the local grocery store.

4. You signed up to serve food and to hand out blankets at a shelter in your community. You drive up and see shivering men, women, and

---

2. Activity idea contributed by Valerie K. Hattery.

children waiting in line. Several of them complain loudly to you about the long wait.

5. A family comes to your office at the church during the week. The father tells you about recently getting out of prison and trying to get back on his feet again. He asks what the church has in place to help him and his family.

6. Your church has agreed to help resettle a group of refugees. You had volunteered to help gather clothing, but at the last minute there is one extra family coming and you have been asked to take them in for two months.

Graffiti Wall[3]

Using large sheets of paper and thick markers, begin a Graffiti Wall. Title the various sheets:

"I would love to help with the strangers in our community but . . ."

"Hospitality is . . ."

"A stranger is . . ."

"Things that make people the same and things that make people different . . ."

Invite group members to write out brief responses. Post the pages at each meeting and continue developing them over the course of the study. Periodically, discuss comments and trends you notice.

Hospitality Interviews

Identify and interview people you know who offer hospitality regularly and with joy. You might ask them about:

How they learned the practice; who were their teachers?

Who they welcome and why?

What they do to make regular hospitality more manageable?

---

3. Activity idea contributed by Valerie K. Hattery.

What they think is the hardest part? The best part?
Be prepared to share the insights from your interviews during the last
week of the study group.

Information Fair[4]

Have the study group sponsor, for your church or for several local
churches, an information fair about volunteer opportunities. Identify organizations for which hospitality to strangers is a significant part of their
work (e.g., homeless shelters, adoption agencies, Big Brother/Big Sister,
refugee organizations, hospice, adult day care). Invite representatives to
come and talk briefly about what they do and how people can volunteer.
Encourage representatives to set up displays and be available to answer
individual questions.

Las Posadas

Within Hispanic communities, *Las Posadas* is a beloved reenactment of
Mary's and Joseph's search for shelter (posadas) on the night that Jesus
was born. If the study is held during Advent, group members might want
to involve their congregations in this ritual. Each night for nine days before Christmas, participants go to the homes of congregation members
asking for shelter. After several experiences of rejection and closed doors,
they find welcome at the last home and all celebrate together. For further
information on this activity, partner with a local Hispanic congregation or
make researching the tradition part of the activity.

Mini-Dramas

Act out one of the biblical stories of hospitality by translating it into a contemporary setting.

---

4. Activity idea contributed by Valerie K. Hattery.

Plan Ahead

Simple preparations make it easier to welcome people into our homes on little notice. Divide into small groups and brainstorm about:

> The kinds of nonperishable or frozen-food items you could have in your house to be able to provide a quick, simple meal.
> Practical suggestions for making hospitality easier (e.g., particular routines, soup on the stove, favorite recipes).

Post-A-Quote

Post paper on the walls around the room. Encourage people to write out simple statements of key insights they are learning as they are going through the study.

Praying for Strangers

As a spiritual discipline, make a practice of praying each night for one stranger you encountered during the day.

For several weeks, make it a point to notice the visitors and strangers who come to your church. Pray for them by name each day. Ask God to open opportunities for hospitality.

Refugee Ministries

Visit a refugee ministry in your area and inquire about what is involved in sponsoring a family. Learn about the work of the agency, the countries from which refugees are coming, and the local churches that are involved with resettlement. Consider how you or your church might become more involved with offering a generous welcome to refugees.

Shared Meals

Because shared meals are such a central part of the hospitality tradition, it is an important part of the learning process to connect meals with conversation during this study. Meals could be part of each meeting or scheduled periodically throughout the study. Individual participants could take turns providing and/or hosting them or each member could bring something to share.

Special Variations

1. Individuals or pairs of group members could invite to dinner four to six people that they don't know well from church. After the first meal, hosts should ask if guests might want to continue eating together on a monthly basis. Be prepared to host the meal a second time but invite others to volunteer to host the subsequent meals. If the menu is simple and inexpensive, food preparation will be less intimidating and distracting, and others will be more likely to participate.

2. Arrange a potluck dinner involving various ethnic dishes. Send group members out the week ahead in pairs to the relevant ethnic stores. Choose recipes that require unusual ingredients. Encourage the shoppers to ask for storeowners' assistance in purchasing the ingredients. During the meal, invite participants to share their experiences of trying to buy and cook with unfamiliar ingredients. How does this experience of shopping and cooking provide insight into the feelings of newly arrived immigrants or refugees as they try to adjust to everyday life in a new land?

3. Begin plans to establish a monthly potluck meal for recently arrived immigrants, migrant workers, or elderly people in your community. Invite a church youth group to help host the meal. Make sure that everyone sits down together to eat.

4. Contact a relief and development agency for directions on how to host a church-wide feast and famine meal (e.g., World Vision's *30 Hour Famine*).

5. One unusual variation of a potluck meal is the "dump" dinner. Prior to the dinner, ask each member of the group to bring a pound of one of the following items: beef, sausage, pork, chicken, seafood and/or fish, potatoes, and larger vegetables (carrots, onions, celery, etc.). Chop meats and vegetables into chunks (make them slightly larger than stew size). Fill a very large pot halfway with water. Bring water to a boil, adding spices (salt, pepper, garlic, bay leaves). Once the water has begun to boil, add the meat. After meat is cooked, add potatoes and vegetables. Finally, add seafood and/or fish. Continue to boil until everything is fully cooked but not mushy. Drain the pot of all liquid.

Prepare a large table by covering it with heavy-duty paper (line with plastic if necessary). Have many napkins, several loaves of bread, and pre-cut individual portions of butter ready. After the soup has been completely drained, carefully dump it directly on the table. Invite everyone to sit down and to dig in (it works best if plates and silverware are NOT available).

Although slightly messy, the meal is a great leveler, surprisingly tasty, and very enjoyable (ingredients can be varied to suit the taste of group members, as long as items are large enough to be handled without silverware). Because cooking time is significant, plan other activities or discussions for that period. One possibility is to read and discuss the following folk tale called "Stone Soup."

STONE SOUP[5]

Once upon a time, somewhere in Eastern Europe, there was a great famine. People jealously hoarded whatever food they could find, hiding it even from their friends and neighbors. One day a peddler drove his wagon into a village, sold a few of his wares, and began asking questions as if he planned to stay for the night.

"There's not a bite to eat in the whole province," he was told. "Better keep moving on."

"Oh, I have everything I need," he said. "In fact, I was thinking of making some stone soup to share with all of you." He pulled an iron

---

5. From http://spanky.triumf.ca/www/fractint/stone_soup.html

cauldron from his wagon, filled it with water, and built a fire under it. Then, with great ceremony, he drew an ordinary-looking stone from a velvet bag and dropped it into the water.

By now, hearing the rumor of food, most of the villagers had come to the square or watched from their windows. As the peddler sniffed the "broth" and licked his lips in anticipation, hunger began to overcome their skepticism.

"Ahh," the peddler said to himself rather loudly, "I do like a tasty stone soup. Of course, stone soup with CABBAGE — that's hard to beat."

Soon a villager approached hesitantly, holding a cabbage he'd retrieved from its hiding place, and added it to the pot. "Capital!" cried the peddler. "You know, I once had stone soup with cabbage and a bit of salt beef as well, and it was fit for a king."

The village butcher managed to find some salt beef . . . and so it went, through potatoes, onions, carrots, mushrooms, and so on, until there was indeed a delicious meal for all. The villagers offered the peddler a great deal of money for the magic stone, but he refused to sell and traveled on the next day. And from that time on, long after the famine had ended, they reminisced about the finest soup they'd ever had.

Stranger Collage[6]

Invite group members to collect pictures of "strangers" (e.g., people different from yourself, "people without a place"). Create a collage from the pictures. Talk about:

How are these people different/similar?

Why do we hesitate to welcome people different from ourselves?

Which types of strangers in the collage particularly need your welcome?

Choose several faces in the collage. Ask yourselves, "If I saw the face of Christ in this person, I would say to him or her . . ."

---

6. Activity idea contributed by Valerie K. Hattery.

Volunteer Experience

Choose to do something together over the duration of the study, such as volunteering at a homeless shelter, food pantry or soup kitchen, refugee agency, group home for people with disabilities, or nursing home. It would be helpful to go as a group so the shared experience can be discussed, but, in some circumstances, the group may need to divide into smaller units.

Reflect on the experience briefly at the study session each week using some of the following questions:

What were your feelings as you worked in the setting?

Did you see expressions of hospitality and inhospitality?

What did you observe about guest/host interactions, power and authority in relationships?

How do the location and the space communicate welcome and respect?

What surprised you? Troubled you?

What are you gaining from this experience?

How do your insights and questions change over time? Why?

Walk around the Walls

Divide into pairs and walk around your church making a note of the signs, directions, and images on the walls. Come back as a group and discuss what they say about the kinds of people that are welcome in your church. What changes might communicate a more inclusive welcome?

VIDEOS

And Then Came John: A Triumph Over Down's Syndrome
(36 minutes, distributed through Filmakers Library [212-804-4960])

This is a story about a winsome young man with Down's syndrome and a family, community, and church that understood the importance and joys of inclusion. John's insights into what it means to be welcomed are "stunning."

1. What did it mean for John to be valued by his family, community, and church? How were the various people in his life affected by him?

2. What do you learn about hospitality and about people with disabilities from John's own comments? What do you learn from his family and friends?

3. Inclusion clearly brings life in this story. Are there situations you know of where a hospitable response to someone who is usually overlooked might be life-giving?

54

Babette's Feast

(102 minutes, available through local video stores)

In this fascinating story, two sisters in a remote Danish village open their home to a needy stranger from France. As Babette cooks for the sisters, she offers them and their strict religious community opportunities to participate in beauty, abundance, and reconciliation. The dialogue of this Academy Award-winning film is in French and Danish, with English subtitles.

1. Discuss the various ways that guest and host roles intertwine and change in the story. For which characters are the reversals important but difficult? Why?

2. In what ways does Babette, as the stranger, both attract and frighten the community? What gifts does she bring to the community? What do community members expect from her?

3. How are the various characters affected by Babette's act of extravagant hospitality?

4. At what points does this story challenge you?

Entertaining Angels: The Dorothy Day Story

(111 minutes, distributed through Gateway Films/Vision Video [800-523-0226])

The challenging story of Dorothy Day and Peter Maurin, this film depicts the founding of the Catholic Worker movement in the 1930s. The film, especially the second half, gives rich insight into the mix of difficulty, heartache, and beauty in the first Catholic Worker House of Hospitality in New York. Viewers gain a glimpse of the tensions and mystery that come with reaching out to homeless people.

1. What did you learn from the film about the continuing tensions between grace and difficulty, hospitality and limited resources?

2. Reflect on the personal costs of offering hospitality to strangers.

3. How was Dorothy Day's relationship with God both tested and shaped by her work with the poor?

Martin the Cobbler

(Claymation, 27 minutes, distributed through Gateway Films/Vision Video [800-523-0226])

The Visitor

(a contemporary adaptation, 30 minutes, distributed through Gateway Films/Vision Video)

Both films are based on Leo Tolstoy's short story, "Where Love Is, God Is." After losing his family, Martin, a cobbler, found little reason to live. But through reading the Scriptures and hearing a voice in a dream, Martin expects the Lord to visit him the following day. He eagerly looks for the Lord's visit but finds himself changed as he responds to a steady stream of needy strangers. He unexpectedly finds the joy of welcoming Jesus in "the least of these."

1. How is Martin changed by the expectation that the Lord would visit him?

2. When does Martin realize that the people he welcomed or cared for were Jesus in disguise?

3. In what ways is Martin also Jesus to them?

4. Who are the people through whom Jesus might come to you? Would you live differently if you thought that God might come to you in the form of a stranger?

Spitfire Grill
(117 minutes, available through local video stores)

When Percy Talbot arrived as a stranger in a small town in Maine, the residents were not sure how to respond to her. *Spitfire Grill* is a beautiful yet disturbing story about welcome and rejection on many levels.

1. Who are the strangers and hosts in the story? How do the townspeople respond to them?

2. Discuss Percy's role as a stranger:
   a. In what ways is she both stranger and host?
   b. What does she bring to the townspeople and to the town itself?
   c. Why is she threatening to them?

3. Try to identify all of the settings for, or incidents of, hospitality and inhospitality in the film.

4. How is the town changed by the stranger in its midst?

The Visitor
*(see **Martin the Cobbler**)*

Weapons of the Spirit
(120 minutes, for distribution information see www.chambon.org)

During World War II, a small Protestant village in the mountains of France sheltered five thousand Jewish refugees. In documentary form, this powerful film tells the story of Le Chambon through interviews with surviving villagers. At the end of the film, Bill Moyers talks with the producer, Pierre Sauvage.

1. How did the villagers explain their hospitality? What struck you about the villagers' character and history — what were they like?

2. Why did the people of Le Chambon think it was "natural" or "normal" to rescue Jews fleeing from the Holocaust when many Christians in Europe turned their backs on the Jews?

3. Why were the people able to resist nonviolently? What biblical texts and historical experiences shaped the villagers' response to strangers?

4. Invite group members to share one insight they gained from the film about a Christian response to vulnerable strangers.

SUGGESTED PRAYERS, HYMNS, AND READINGS

PRAYERS

Lord Jesus, be our holy guest,
Our morning joy, our evening rest;
And with our daily bread impart
Your love and peace to every heart. Amen.

Book of Common Worship[7]

Our Father, we rejoice in the guests who sit at meat with us, for our food is the more welcome because they share it, and our home the dearer because it shelters them. Grant that in the happy exchange of thought and affection we may realize anew that all our gladness

---

7. *The Book of Common Worship* (Louisville: Westminster/John Knox Press, 1993), Prayers at Mealtime #11, p. 594.

comes from the simple fellowship of our human kind, and that we
are rich as long as we are loved.

Walter Rauschenbusch[8]

Open my eyes that they may see
the deepest needs of people;
Move my hands that they may feed the hungry;
Touch my heart that it may bring warmth to the despairing;
Teach me the generosity that welcomes strangers;
Let me share my possessions to clothe the naked;
Give me the care that strengthens the sick;
Make me share in the quest to set the prisoner free.
In sharing our anxieties and our love,
our poverty and our prosperity,
we partake of your divine presence.

Canaan Banana, Zimbabwe[9]

We bring before you, O Lord, the troubles and perils of people and
nations, the sighing of prisoners and captives, the sorrows of the bereaved, the necessities of strangers, the helplessness of the weak, the
despondency of the weary, the failing powers of the aged. O Lord,
draw near to each; for the sake of Jesus Christ our Lord. Amen.

St. Anselm (1033-1109)[10]

Make us worthy, Lord,
to serve our fellow human beings throughout the world
who live and die in poverty and hunger.

8. Walter Rauschenbusch, *Prayers of the Social Awakening* (Boston: The Pil-
grim Press, 1910), 41-42.

9. *With All God's People: The New Ecumenical Prayer Cycle* (Geneva: WCC
Publications, 1989), 344.

10. Horton Davies, ed., *The Communion of Saints: Prayers of the Famous*
(Grand Rapids: Wm. B. Eerdmans, 1990), 124.

Give them through our hands, this day their daily bread,
and by our understanding love,
give peace and joy. Amen.

Mother Teresa of Calcutta[11]

O God, who created all peoples in your image, we thank you for the wonderful diversity of races and cultures in this world. Enrich our lives by ever-widening circles of fellowship, and show us your presence in those who differ most from us, until our knowledge of your love is made perfect in our love for all your children; through Jesus Christ our Lord. Amen.

Book of Common Prayer[12]

God of grace,
no one is beyond the reach of your love,
or outside your limitless mercy.
Move us toward those the world despises and people reject,
so we may venture to follow Christ,
and risk showing his love.
Stand with those who are outcast;
strengthen them in peace;
encourage them by your presence;
and use them to build on the cornerstone of Christ,
until differences are honored and respected,
and all people together give you glory. Amen.

Book of Common Worship[13]

---

11. Excerpted from *Lord Hear Our Prayer,* ed. by Thomas McNally, C.S.C., and William Storey, D.M.S. Copyright © 2000 by Ave Maria Press, P.O. Box 428, Notre Dame, IN 46556, www.avemariapress.com. Used with permission of the publisher.

12. *The Book of Common Prayer* (New York: Oxford University Press, 1979), Prayers and Thanksgivings, Thanksgiving #7, p. 840.

13. *The Book of Common Worship,* Litanies and Prayers for Various Occasions #115, p. 834.

Almighty and most merciful God, we remember before you all poor and neglected persons whom it would be easy for us to forget: the homeless and the destitute, the old and the sick, and all who have none to care for them. Help us to heal those who are broken in body or spirit, and to turn their sorrow into joy. Grant this, Father, for the love of your Son, who for our sake became poor, Jesus Christ our Lord. Amen.

Book of Common Prayer[14]

Jesus, make our hearts ever gentler and more humble,
so that we may be present to those you have confided to our care,
and in this way make us instruments of your love
which gives life and joy and real freedom.

Jean Vanier, Canada[15]

PRAYERS OF CONFESSION

Lord, we confess our day to day failure to be truly human.
Lord, we confess to you.
Lord, we confess that we often fail to love with all we have and are,
often because we do not fully understand what loving means,
often because we are afraid of risking ourselves.
Lord, we confess to you.
Lord, we cut ourselves off from each other and we erect barriers of division.
Lord, we confess to you.
Lord, we confess that by silence and ill-considered word
we have built up walls of prejudice.
Lord, we confess that by selfishness and lack of sympathy
we have stifled generosity and left little time for others.

---

14. *The Book of Common Prayer,* Prayers and Thanksgivings, Prayer #35, p. 826.
15. *With All God's People,* 225.

Holy Spirit, speak to us. Help us listen to your word of forgiveness, for we are very deaf. Come, fill this moment and free us from sin.

United Methodist Hymnal[16]

My Prayer

O God,
you have sown the seeds of love in my heart
but I have not watered it with my tears —
Lord forgive.

You have shown me hungry children
and I have fed only my friends —
Lord forgive.

You have shown me the homeless
and I have cared only for my own home —
Lord forgive.

You have shown me the naked
but I have only clothed myself —
Lord forgive.

You have shown me the wounded
and I have been only concerned with my own pain —
Lord forgive.

You have shown me the friendless
and I have nurtured my own friendships —
Lord forgive.

---

16. *The United Methodist Hymnal* (Nashville: The United Methodist Publishing House, 1989), Prayer of Confession #893.

You have shown me the bereaved
and I have sought out others to comfort me —
Lord forgive.

You have shown me those who do not know your love
and I have failed to share that which you have given me —
Lord forgive and help me to obey.

Ethel Jenkins[17]

HYMNS   *(titles or first lines)*

Help us accept each other as Christ accepted us
Here I Am, Lord
I'm a-Going to Eat at the Welcome Table
Jesu, Jesu, fill us with your love
Lord whose love through humble service
One bread, one body, one Lord of all

READINGS

Isaiah 58:6-9
Psalm 146
Matthew 25:31-46
Romans 12:9-21

Where charity and love prevail,
there God is ever found;
brought here together by Christ's love,
by love are we thus bound.
. . . .

---

17. Geoffrey Duncan, ed., *Dare to Dream: A Prayer and Worship Anthology from Around the World* (Harper Collins, 1995), 57.

Love can exclude no race or creed
If honored be God's name;
our common life embraces all
whose Maker is the same.

9th century Latin hymn[18]

We saw a stranger yesterday.
We put food in the eating place,
Drink in the drinking place,
Music in the listening place,
And with the sacred name of the triune God
He blessed us and our house,
Our cattle and our dear ones.
As the lark says in her song:
Often, often, often, goes the Christ
In the stranger's guise.

Celtic Rune of Hospitality

True evangelical faith
   cannot lie dormant
   it clothes the naked
   it feeds the hungry
   it comforts the sorrowful
   it shelters the destitute
   it serves those that harm it
   it binds up that which is wounded
   it has become all things to all creatures.

Menno Simmons, 16th century[19]

Come, sinners, to the gospel feast;
let every soul be Jesus' guest.
Ye need not one be left behind,
for God hath bid all humankind.

---

18. English text by Omer Westendorf. Copyright © 1960, World Library Publications, Schiller Park, IL. Alt. Used by permission.
19. *With All God's People,* 131.

. . . .

Come, all ye souls by sin oppressed,
ye restless wanderers after rest;
ye poor, and maimed, and halt, and blind,
in Christ a hearty welcome find.

Charles Wesley, 18th century[20]

You have come from afar
and waited long and are wearied:
Let us sit side by side
sharing the same bread drawn from the same source
to quiet the same hunger that makes us weak.
Then standing together
let us share the same spirit, the same thoughts
that once again draw us together in friendship
    and unity and peace.

Prières d'Ozawamick, Native American[21]

Is it enough?

Face to face we sit —
the silence, like a stone wall,
separating us.

It is not enough
to sit in proximity
if we have no trust.

Give us hearts of flesh
to grieve our hostility:
then grant us laughter

---

20. *The United Methodist Hymnal*, #339.
21. *With All God's People*, 223.

and let us reach out.
Even if we do not see
eye to eye clearly

dare us open up
our hands, be hospitable:
bare us, soul to soul.

                                                    Kate Compston[22]

---

22. Duncan, ed., *Dare to Dream,* 143.